# Daniel's Choices

Written by:
**JOANNE HUGHES**

Illustrated by:
**CHERRI LOW HORN**

**Trafford**
PUBLISHING®  www.trafford.com

**North America & international**
toll-free: 1 888 232 4444 (USA & Canada)
fax: 812 355 4082

For my children and children everywhere,
to my family for their wisdom, strength and encouragement,
to my loving partner for all your support.....

It is my intent that this book get into the hands of children
everywhere, caregivers, educators,doctors and mental health systems.
I have met many children who have thought of suicide at least once in
their life....I hope this book gets them and everyone talking
so that kids never have to feel alone.

Daniel Saunders was a typical 10-year-old child, at least most would think so. But there was another side to him that nobody knew about … until recently. Daniel wasn't into sports like most boys his age, but liked to hang out with his friends and skateboard or ride his bike. He wasn't an 'A' student although he did pretty well. Daniel had an older brother named Steve. Steve was 14, an honor role student, popular, and very good at all sports. In fact, every time that Steve played a game, his parents were always there to cheer him on. Daniel felt left out and as though he was invisible.

Daniel began to struggle. His grades, which were average to begin with, began to drop. He was sent home for fighting on two occasions and things just seemed to get worse and worse.

One day, when Daniel arrived home from school, he threw down his coat and backpack and headed to the upstairs bathroom. He looked in the mirror and thought, "Great, how am I going to hide this?" He wiped away blood from his lip; he had been in another fight.

Daniel knew the school would be calling and he felt scared and worried about how his parents would react to this. He went to the kitchen and found a note.

*"We're at Steve's soccer game. There is leftover meatloaf*
*in the fridge. We'll be back around 8:00 p.m. tonight.*
*Mom*

"Meatloaf again?" he groaned. Daniel grabbed his coat and headed off to Paul's house.

When Daniel got to his friend's house, Paul's mom answered the door. "Oh my, what happened to you?" she exclaimed.

"Fight," Daniel muttered as he stared down at his feet.

"Paul is down at the skateboard park," said Paul's mom.

"Thanks. Gotta go." Daniel turned and left quickly, heading down to the skateboard park. "Hey Danny, what happened to your face?" cried Paul running towards Daniel.

"Kyle was bugging me again. I asked him to stop or he'd get it. He never listened, so I hit him. I'm tired of getting pushed around!"

"Well, at least you showed him! Maybe he won't bug you any more now."

"Well, I sure hope not. I'm tired of fighting," grumbled Daniel.

Paul and Daniel talked for a while. Daniel told Paul he was scared that his dad would be really upset with him and he would probably be grounded for a month. "My dad is always telling me I should be more like Steve; Steve this, Steve that, Steve, Steve, Steve! Man, Steve **always** gets the good grades,

dad's **constantly** taking him on fishing trips with him, and he never takes me! I wish I were dead! Then I'd show them! They'd wish they treated me better then!" Suddenly, Paul felt sick in his stomach.

"Daniel, what are you talking about?" asked Paul.

"Never mind!" replied Daniel.

Daniel picked up his coat and headed home. It was dark now and his parents would be wondering where he was.

As Daniel came in the door, he heard his parents arguing. "Oh man, not again!" he thought to himself. Daniel tried to sneak quietly up to his room but his dad saw him.

"Where do you think you are going?" called Mr. Saunders. Daniel kept walking. "GET IN HERE NOW!" shouted his dad.

Daniel went to the living room, his palms sweaty and his stomach feeling tight. "What happened?" gasped his mom. "Were you in another fight?"

"Yeah," said Daniel as he looked at the ground.

"Oh great!" yelled Mr. Saunders. "You had better not get suspended or you will be grounded! When will you learn?" Daniel felt scared as his dad was pretty angry. Daniel ran up to his room and closed the door. He threw everything off his desk, sat down and pounded his fists on the desk.

"Why can't they just listen to me? Why don't they understand?"

Daniel's parents continued to argue downstairs as they had many times before. Daniel felt hopeless, unheard, misunderstood and unloved. He wiped away his tears and decided to go into his brother's room. Steve had heard the fighting and knew, from past experience, to stay away. Steve had his headphones on and didn't hear Daniel enter the room.

Daniel tapped Steve on the shoulder and Steve turned quickly with his fist in the air. "What do you want?" Steve snapped.

"Can I talk to you?" pleaded Daniel.

"Do you think I want to talk now?" snarled Steve. "You're probably the reason why they're fighting." So Daniel, feeling hurt, turned and ran back to his room.

He slammed his bedroom door and said, "I'll show you. I'll show all of you!" He sat at his desk and began to write a suicide note. At that moment in time Daniel felt very alone. He thought nobody loved or cared about him and that it would be better if he ended his life.

Daniel was up early the next morning. He had thought a lot about his note and about how and when he would end his life. He gathered some of his favorite things; some music CDs and the one and only trophy he got when he played peewee hockey. He stopped and looked at the trophy and, for a brief moment, a big smile crossed his face. Things were good back then. His dad had been proud of him playing hockey. When he won that trophy his dad had run up to him, hugged him and put him up on his shoulders. Daniel's smile turned to a frown and tears began to run down his cheek. "Why can't he be proud of me now, just the way I am?" he wailed.

Daniel felt angry now. He put the trophy in his bag and went downstairs. His dad had already left for work and his mom was putting dishes away.

As Daniel grabbed his lunch bag out of the fridge, his mom turned to him and asked, "Daniel, is something wrong, sweetie?" Daniel paused and looked at his mom. He wanted to say something but was afraid to.

"No," said Daniel, "I have to get to school." Mrs. Saunders looked concerned as she watched her son leave the house.

"Mom …" started Daniel.

"What is it?" asked Mrs. Saunders.

"I …" Daniel began, "never mind," and he turned and left.

Daniel arrived at school early and found Paul outside on the playground. "Hey, Paul!" yelled Daniel. Paul saw his friend and ran over to him.

"Hey, Paul, I have something for you," Daniel said, putting his backpack down.

"What is it?" inquired Paul. Daniel took out his prized hockey trophy and handed it to Paul.

"What are you doing with that?" Paul asked.

"I want you to have this; you're my best friend," Daniel said. Paul looked puzzled but remembered what Daniel had told him the night before about wishing that he were dead.

"Daniel," said Paul, "this is your hockey trophy and you would never part with this. What's going on?"

"Nothing!" snapped Daniel. "You are my best friend and I want you to have it. I can take it back if you want!"

"Well no-o," replied Paul "it's just …"

Daniel picked up his backpack and walking off saying, "Just take care of it, okay?" Paul stood there, trophy in hand. He knew something wasn't right.

Just then the bell rang. The boys ran inside and went to their classroom. Paul took his seat next to Daniel. They had a surprise test that day; Daniel hadn't been studying lately and didn't understand the questions. He stood up, angrily threw down his pencil, picked up his backpack and ran out the door. The teacher, Mrs. Smith, wanted to go after him but knew he needed some space. She looked down and saw a crumpled piece of paper. She picked it up, put it in her pocket and went to her desk. "Time up!" she said. The tests were collected and the bell rang.

Paul remained in his seat after the bell rang. Mrs. Smith turned and saw him sitting there. "Paul, can I help you?" Paul shifted in his seat feeling uncomfortable. "Paul?" Mrs. Smith called one more time.

"Well," Paul began, "I'm worried about Daniel."

"What do you mean?" asked Mrs. Smith.

Paul told Mrs. Smith about the fight Daniel was in the day before and the fighting at Daniel's house and what Daniel had said about wanting to be dead and how that would be better for him.

Mrs. Smith smiled at Paul and said, "Thanks for telling me! That was very brave of you. This is really serious and Daniel needs some help right now."

Paul admitted he was feeling scared for Daniel and wanted to tell someone. Then he left the room to try to find his friend.

Mrs. Smith took the note that fell out of Daniel's backpack, opened it and read it. It read:

*Dear Mom and Dad,*

*I know I've been the reason for you guys fighting and I know you wished you had a different son. I'm going to end this all now and things will get better. I'm sorry for everything I've done.*

*I love you Mom and Dad. Say bye to Steve for me.*

*Daniel*

Mrs. Smith was very alarmed and ran to the school counselor's office to show him what she had found. Mr. Brand read the note and asked where Daniel was. Mrs. Smith explained what happened in class and about Paul and her talk with him. Mr. Brand picked up the phone to call Daniel's parents and ask them to come in right away.

Meanwhile, Paul had found Daniel in the boys' washroom. "Daniel, what are you doing in here?" Paul asked.

"Nothing, leave me alone!" Daniel cried, tears streaming down his cheeks. "There's nothing anybody can do now, go away!"

Paul began talking to Daniel in a calm, quiet voice, hoping that he could get Daniel's mind off his troubles. He talked about all the fun things they had done in the past and what they would do this summer.

"DANIEL SAUNDERS, PLEASE REPORT TO THE
FRONT OFFICE, DANIEL SAUNDERS…
TO THE FRONT OFFICE, PLEASE."

Daniel stood up and said, "I have to go, Paul." Daniel went to Paul and hugged him.

**"No, Daniel!"** Paul shouted, "You have to go to the office!" Daniel began to walk out and Paul yelled, "Daniel, are you thinking of suicide?" Paul swallowed, feeling uncomfortable with his question.

Daniel stopped, turned around and confessed, "Y-yes, I am."

"Daniel, go talk to the counselor, please," pleaded Paul. "I'll go with you, if that helps." Daniel nodded his head and wiped away a tear. Deep inside, Daniel wanted help but hadn't known how to ask for it. He felt relieved now that someone knew. The boys headed off to the counselor's office and sat down outside.

Meanwhile, Mr. Brand had phoned Daniel's mom. He told Mrs. Saunders that Mrs. Smith had found a note from Daniel that was quite disturbing and that she and her husband needed to come to the school immediately. Mrs. Saunders felt panicked as she hung up the phone. She remembered how she had felt that something wasn't quite right with Daniel that morning and she began to worry as the events of the past months began to flash through her mind.

She thought about Daniel's marks falling, his fighting more at school and his isolation from his family. Mrs. Saunders grabbed her coat and purse and rushed out to the car. Her hands were shaking and her heart racing as she took out her cell phone and dialed her husband's number at work. It seemed

ages before he answered, "Kyle Saunders speaking." Her voice cracked as she called out, "Kyle, we have to get to the school right away!" Mr. Saunders could hear the concern in his wife's voice.

"Hold on now! Tell me what is wrong. Start at the beginning. Did Daniel get in trouble for fighting again?" Mr. Saunders asked.

"No, something is wrong!" Mrs. Saunders cried out. "The counselor called me this morning and told me that he had a note that Daniel had written and that it was quite disturbing. When Daniel left this morning I just felt that something was wrong, he was acting so differently. I'm on my way there now."

"Okay, I'm on my way, too," replied Mr. Saunders.

Daniel's parents arrived at the school at the same time and were met by Mr.

Brand. They were shown the note and talked about what was happening at home and how they would approach this with Daniel.

Meanwhile, Daniel and Paul were waiting outside the counselor's office. Daniel was sitting with his head resting on his hands, his eyes wet from tears. The office door opened. "Come on in, Daniel," invited Mr. Brand. Mr. and Mrs. Saunders were already sitting in the office when Daniel came in.

"Daniel, we love you so much. How could you think like this?" cried his mom.

Mr. Brand interrupted, "Daniel, we found your suicide note; it seems you've been feeling pretty bad lately. We want to help."

Daniel's dad lowered his head and raised his hand up to his eye, wiping away

a tear. He looked over at Mr. Brand. The room fell silent … you could hear a pin drop.

Mr. Brand spoke, shattering the silence, "Things can be pretty hard sometimes. We can feel a lot of pressure these days – in our home life, our school life and, even more so, in our social life with our friends. We want to help you feel better and to give you better ways of dealing with everyday pressure and stress. We want to help, Daniel."

Daniel began to talk and, even though it felt uncomfortable, he told his parents and Mr. Brand how he had been feeling lately. Daniel told his parents how he hated it when they fought. He felt so scared when they argued, and Steve hated it too. Daniel said that he had wanted to phone the police many times but that he was afraid that the police would take him away. He spoke of how his dad made him feel that Steve was better than him. Daniel let years of anger and sadness come out and, in doing so, felt like the world had just been lifted off his shoulders.

Mr. Saunders started to speak, his face flushed red and his voice cracking, "I'm sorry, Daniel. We never meant for you to be afraid. Your mom and I have had some problems lately but we're willing to get some help."

Mr. Brand walked over to Daniel and put a hand on his shoulder. "You know, Daniel, I understand how you must have been feeling but suicide should never be an option. I'd like to make a contract with you. Let's talk about other things you can do when you're feeling bad. Okay?"

Daniel, Mr. Brand and his parents all began to think of choices. Mr. Saunders apologized again, "I'm sorry, Daniel. I will try to listen to you more and I

guess we need to spend more time together if I'm going to understand you better."

"You see, Daniel," said Mr. Brand, "we all have choices. There are good and bad choices. You can always talk to someone when you're feeling down. Who are some people you can talk to?"

Daniel thought about it and said "Well, I can talk to you, and I can talk to Paul, too; he understands me."

"You can talk to us too, son," added his dad.

"Good," said Mr. Brand. "Now you have a list of people to talk to when you're feeling down. Now let's think about what you can do when you're upset."

"Daniel," said his mom, "you love to skateboard. Maybe you could take your dad and me down to the park and show us how you skateboard. That's one thing you can do." Mrs. Saunders thought some more. "And we will get you some help with your math if you're having trouble."

"Good idea!" said Mr. Brand.

Mr. Brand turned to Daniel, "I've given your parents some phone numbers that they can call so that you can all go and talk to a counselor.

"A counselor is someone you can trust who will listen to you and help you work things out. There are good programs where you can talk to a counselor as a family, as this affects all of you."

Mr. Brand sat back down at his desk and got out a piece of paper. "Daniel, let's sign this contract between you and I now. This is an agreement between us that says that you will talk to me or another counselor if you ever feel like hurting yourself again. You could make up a contract with your parents at home as well. What do you all think about that?"

"I can do that," said Daniel.

"We will do one as soon as we get home, as well." agreed Daniel's mom. "Now that all this is out in the open, we can begin to work on things."

Daniel and his parents shook Mr. Brand's hand. "Thanks," said Daniel "for everything."

Paul was still waiting outside the office when Daniel came out. "We'll wait down here," said Mrs. Saunders.

Daniel walked slowly over to his friend. "Paul, I-I just wanted to say thanks, thanks for caring and thanks for being my friend. I know now that I have choices. When I'm upset, suicide is never a choice."

"Glad to hear you say that, I would have been bored all summer!" laughed Paul.

Mrs. Saunders hugged Paul. "I'm so glad Daniel has a friend like you! Thank you so much!"

Daniel's mom turned to Daniel and said, "It will be a lot of work and it will take time, but it's a start. And I think we all will have to make different choices from now on."

Daniel and David walked down the hall laughing and planning their weekend. Daniel felt better inside. He was glad that he was wrong about his parents not loving him.

Suicide is a very devastating and final decision. You always have choices. Remember, you are NEVER alone. Talk to someone you trust and tell them how you are feeling. Get help.

Write down some things you can do when you are feeling bad, e.g. color, listen to music, and call your friends.

_____

_____

_____

_____

_____

_____

Who are people you can talk to when you're feeling sad or feel like hurting yourself?

_____

_____

_____

_____

_____

_____

**Kids' Help Line – 1-800-668-6868**

**Joanne Hughes** worked in the field of domestic violence as a Child Support Counsellor for over 15 years. She enjoyed running groups, working one to one with women and children and always loved seeing their smiles and courage. Joanne currently resides in British Columbia with her partner and children and is running a retreat and wellness center.

**Cherri Low Horn**, a member of the Siksika Nation Tribe in southern Alberta, was born and raised in Calgary, Alberta, Canada. In 2002 she graduated with a B.A. from the University of Calgary. In 2003 she studied First Nation Art at the Institute of American Indian Arts in Santa Fe, New Mexico.

Since 1997 Cherri has worked with Aboriginal youth and their families, both on and off First Nation's Reservations. In 2004 she began to work with Native, and non-Native, families dealing with domestic violence and poverty under the Awo Taan Native Women Shelter Society, as a Child Support Worker. Cherri met Joanne in 2005 at the Calgary Women's Emergency Shelter in the Child Support Program.

Cherri has been an active member in recognizing First Nation issues. In 2002 she helped on the World Indigenous People's Conference on Education, organized out of Treaty 7. In the 2005 Cherri was an Advance Team Member and Ceremonial site Organizer under Veteran's Affair Canada in the 2005 Calling Home Ceremony, held in France and Belgium.

Cherri is a published poet (Fish Head Soup: Neo-Modern Native Literature from the Institute of American Indian Art, 2005), and she was also featured in Calgary's local aboriginal youth magazine, New Tribe (January 2006).

Cherri currently resides in Montreal, Quebec where she is pursuing her ambitions in art and multimedia.

Ekuskini@hotmail.com